WINTER BLESSINGS

PATRICIA SCANLAN

Thoughts and Poems to Warm Your Heart

Winter Blessings

HODDER
HEADLINE
IRELAND

First published in Ireland in 2005 by
HODDER HEADLINE IRELAND
8 Castlecourt Centre, Castleknock, Dublin 15, Ireland

First published in the UK in 2005 by
HEADLINE BOOK PUBLISHING

1

Cataloguing in Publication Data is available from
the British Library

ISBN 0 7553 1442 5

Typeset in Bembo and OptiBauer
by Ben Cracknell Studios
Printed and bound in Great Britain by
Mackays of Chatham plc, Chatham, Kent

Hodder Headline's policy is to use papers that are
natural, renewable and recyclable products and made
from wood grown in sustainable forests. The logging
and manufacturing processes are expected to conform
to the environmental regulations of the country
of origin.

HODDER HEADLINE IRELAND
A division of Hodder Headline
338 Euston Road
London NW1 3BH

www.hhireland.ie
www.hodderheadline.com

I dedicate this book, with love and affection, to Ciara Considine, my friend, editor and colleague, whose kind editing and constant reassurance made the writing of this book such a pleasure and without whom I possibly could never have written it.

Dear Ciara, thank you.

CONTENTS

ACKNOWLEDGEMENTS

How could I not thank Jesus, Mary, Saint Joseph, Saint Michael and Saint Anthony, and all my angels, saints and guides, for the inspiration for this book?

To Breda Purdue and all my colleagues at HHI, thanks for publishing it.

To Ruth Shern, for all the enthusiasm and kindness.

To Claire Rourke, a firm but kind editor, who is now a friend.

To Martin Neild, Val Hudson, Jo Roberts-Miller and all at Headline.

To Aidan Storey, who introduced me to the ascended masters and sent me continuous Love and Light.

To Margaret Neylon, who offered constant encouragement and angelic advice.

To my family. Thanks for a great childhood and wonderful memories.

INTRODUCTION

Last year I was working with a wonderful teacher, Niall MacMonagle, on a poetry anthology for people with literacy difficulties. I came upon poems that I had learned at school and it was a delight to reread those old, familiar lines through the eyes of an adult, and not those of a schoolgirl who had to study them. The more I read, the more I remembered. Afterwards, some lines from

'London Snow' by Robert Bridges lingered in my head:

> When men were all asleep the snow came flying,
> In large white flakes falling on the city brown,
> Stealthily and perpetually settling and loosely lying,
> Hushing the latest traffic of the drowsy town...

Before long, snippets from once-memorised poems were coming to mind, such as these evocative, unforgettable lines from Shakespeare's much-loved poem, 'Winter':

> When icicles hang by the wall,
> And Dick the shepherd blows his nail,
> And Tom bears logs into the hall,
> And milk comes frozen home in pail...

One of my favourite poems of all time is 'The Old Woman of the Roads' by Padraic Colum. I always remember these lines vividly:

> Oh, to have a little house!
> To own the hearth and stool and all!
> The heaped-up sods against the fire,
> The pile of turf against the wall!

The loneliness of the old woman on her search for shelter from the harsh weather, and her desire to have her own little house, always resonated strongly with me. I love the description of her imaginary home and the idea of her being snug and safe after her long search. To think that God would answer her prayer and reward her faith in Him gave me hope that He would answer my prayers too.

Having a home of our own is a goal we all strive to achieve: home is a place of refuge, it offers shelter from the storm. To me, the image of the pile of turf beside a cosy fire represents the ultimate protection from the harsh winter weather.

With my new-found delight in these old favourite poems, I went in search of my well-thumbed school textbook, *Exploring English*. It was the one school-book that I had kept, but I couldn't remember where it was. Good old St Anthony, patron saint of lost items, came to the rescue and I found it in my mother's bookcase. It was such a treat to find it and read it again, with all the scribbles and notations of my schooldays taking me right back to my desk in the third row, fourth line down. I remembered the hard wooden chairs, the smell of chalk dust and the drowsy heat of the classroom as the rain battered against the big sash windows.

I've always loved easy, accessible poetry that allows the imagination to run riot. Esoteric, unwieldy poems that I have to struggle to understand never give me pleasure. I wanted to immerse myself again in the poems of my schooldays.

Over a lunchtime discussion with my colleagues at Hodder Headline Ireland, I came up with the idea of putting together an anthology of winter poetry. They were enthusiastic. We talked of winter, of its hardships and joys and of the short days and long nights that most of us dread. We also talked about the certain knowledge that spring will come and the earth will renew itself. This promise of renewal at the heart of winter has the power to transform the darkness of this challenging season into light. As we talked more, the idea for the book began to expand beyond poetry and into recollections, thoughts and blessings that I have experienced over the years. It seemed comforting to explore how winter, the season that is so often a metaphor for negativity in our lives, can also be a symbol of hope. And in that session, the idea for

Winter Blessings was conceived and soon took on a life of its own.

I began to think of my life as though it were divided into seasons. Over the past decade, I have often felt as though I was going through a very long and difficult winter. And yet, in these times of trouble, I was showered with many, many blessings and taken on a spiritual journey that has been deeply enriching. Winter, I now realise, has represented the most meaningful season in my life.

In the mid-nineties, I developed back problems which came to a head one cold, miserable November. A shattered disc left me in agony, barely able to walk. On top of this, I was under great stress in my professional life because of problems with my then publisher. And, to add to my woes, a relationship had ended, at what seemed like the worst time imaginable. Not only was I shattered physically, I was shattered spiritually and emotionally. As I lay in bed, drugged with very strong painkillers, and waiting for a hospital bed, I had never felt so alone. I wondered why this was happening to me. How could God heap all these punishments upon me? What had I done to deserve them?

Yet I knew that this kind of thinking wasn't going to help me. In recent years I had been travelling on a path of spiritual discovery and, for me, new thinking. I began to recognise that we are here to learn lessons in life that give our souls great opportunities for growth. Some of these are learned through joy; others, like the one I was experiencing at the time, are learned through hardship and difficulty.

I had read many books that had radically changed my thinking about religion. I'd moved away from the rigid, authoritative strictures of the religion I'd grown up with and opened myself to a new experience that offered unconditional love and encouragement on my path of searching and seeking. I no longer thought that I was an unworthy, flawed being. I discovered that I, like every other human being on this planet, was a great and magnificent soul on a journey of development and advancement. The books I read were varied, from the eye-opening *Conversations with God* series to the beautiful, deeply profound White Eagle books. I read books about Tibetan Buddhism, books on the ascended masters — Jesus, Buddha, Muhammad and many more – and many books on angels. I learned to try to live in the moment as opposed to fretting about the future or regretting the past. It was a fascinating process: just when I was ready for something new, the right book or teacher would appear.

I remember being at a launch in a bookshop and noticing the new book by Paulo Coelho, *The Alchemist*. I must buy that, I thought. Picking it up, I scanned the back cover and put it back on the shelf. I'd come back to it – I was up to my eyes at the time and decided to buy it when things had calmed down and my current novel was written.

I turned to walk away and the book fell to the floor. I picked it up, replaced it on the shelf and turned to walk away again. Once more it fell. For the third time I replaced it and turned away. Something hit me on the head. The book. I started to laugh. I was meant to read that book now rather than later, and because I had been ignoring the message I had literally been hit on the head with it. I bought it and read it in two days. It was a powerful book about a journey of self-discovery, in which the young shepherd, the main character, discovers that the treasure he is seeking is within.

I had received various types of healing for my back and always noticed that the healers would light a candle and call in many beautiful names to the healing. Some I was familiar with, such as the Master, Jesus; Mary, the beloved Mother; Archangels Michael and Raphael. Others, such as Saint Germain, Mother Meera, Lord Maitreya, Sai Baba, Kuthumi, I had never heard of. I read up on them and found that they were known as ascended masters and avatars, who are helping mankind through the ages to find our divinity and the essence of who we really are.

I learned that an ascended master is a great healer, teacher and prophet who has once lived an earthly life and knows and understands our human difficulties. They have been recognised, in their varying forms, in all the major religions, civilisations and cultures down the ages. Jesus, Buddha, Muhammad and all the angels and saints, deities and devas are here with us to help us when we ask. I learnt that our free will is never interfered with and they come to us *only* if we ask.

All of this I had read and I believed it, yet as I lay in my bed, feeling dejected and in pain, it seemed hard to reconcile my beliefs with my circumstances.

Who would come and help *me*? I wondered. Was all this stuff pie in the sky? Was there really anybody out there or were we all on our own to suffer our hardships and get on with life as best we could?

Several years previously I had been throwing out an old church calendar. On the front of it there was a most beautiful picture of Jesus. He was smiling and serene, so unlike many of the representations of Him in His agony. It seemed disrespectful to throw it in the bin, so I tore it off the front of the calendar, put it in a drawer beside my bed and promptly forgot about it. When I came upon it during a house move a few years later, I took it with me. And now, all those years later, as I railed at what I perceived as God's harshness towards me, I remembered that picture and managed to find it.

'Why, Lord, why?' I asked in deep despair as I stared at the picture, willing answers to come to me. Jesus's eyes seemed so gentle and full of compassion and, for a moment, I was enveloped by a sensation of warmth and calmness and I knew with complete certainty that I was not, had never been, nor ever would be, alone. His presence was so strong and reassuring that I soon fell into a deep sleep, the kind which had eluded me over the past four months of pain and discomfort.

It was another turning-point in my life and the continuation of a journey that is still unfolding. The last ten years were ones of great physical pain and disability, as I traipsed in and out of hospital for a succession of treatments for my back. I was literally brought to my knees. As I recovered from that first operation ten years ago, I read even more spiritual and metaphysical books in an effort to find out why my life was as it was, and to try to uncover my life's purpose. Many of these books spoke of how we have to be stripped to our core and broken in order to be made whole; to experience the dark night of the soul to get to the light. I realised that, if I hadn't been in that wintry place, I would never have developed further on my spiritual path. I would never have come to have deep knowledge of the compassion and unconditional love of Jesus and God and all the wonderful angels and saints and masters who are there for us if we want them to be. I learned that they are longing to help if only we can bring ourselves to ask. I learned that we are all of the Divine. A beach is made up of billions of grains of sand, but those individual grains make up the whole, just as every soul on this planet is part of the One that is All. I began to try to honour the divinity of each person. No one is greater or lesser than any other. We are *all* equal. I learned to try hard not to make judgements. Each of us is on our own path and has made our contract with God.

It became clear that not judging others is the hardest thing to achieve. We make judgements every minute of our lives. Being far from perfect, and despite my best efforts, I can assure you this is not easy and I am constantly reproaching myself for my lack of compassion and humanity. But at least I am aware and try to make an effort.

But I never considered myself 'ill' for those ten years. I call them my years of 'pain-ness' rather than 'illness', and many doors have opened to me because of that time of difficulty. In her wonderful book, *The Game of Life and How to Play It*, Florence Scovel-Shinn gives us the old saying, 'No man is your enemy, no man is your friend, every man is your teacher.' Many healers and teachers have come into my life and given me precious gifts. The gift of love of family and friends, the gift of coming into spiritual knowledge, the gift of trying not to judge myself harshly as well as trying not to judge others.

And so, dear reader, I came to write this book to share some of the gifts that I was given and to bring back memories through the gift of poetry. I lit my candles, as I always do when I'm writing, and asked all my angels, saints and guides for inspiration. And how helpful they were. Lovely, well-remembered poems came my way, as did some delightful new ones.

Beautiful blessings and spiritual writings gave me food for thought. As you read this book, snuggled up cosily on a wintry evening, I hope that all these poems and blessings bring you joy and happy memories, that your heart is warmed and that love and all good things fill your life.

Patricia Scanlan
June 2005

Part One

WINTER

In the depth of winter, I finally realised that within me lay an invincible summer.

Albert Camus

WINTER BLESSINGS

While recuperating from painful major back surgery eighteen months ago, when I'd had a bone graft and screws inserted as a last effort to sort out my back problems, there were times when I got depressed and disheartened, wondering if I would ever be 'normal' again. I was trying to write a novel and, although it was in my head and I was eager to write, the poor recovering body could take only so much punishment at the computer.

One night I was feeling particularly down and was questioning why I was still in bits after all these years, and what value this hardship could possibly have. Surely, I reasoned, it made much more sense for me to use the talents that had been given to me, instead of lying down doing nothing? I picked up a spiritual book that I'd been drawn to and asked for guidance and an answer to my questions. I opened it at random and read a most inspiring passage. The answer I was given couldn't have been clearer. It made me understand that we're often very hard on ourselves. Our treadmills seem to get faster and faster. We need to stop and rest and reflect. Our spirits and our bodies need to renew themselves, just as the earth needs to rest and renew itself over the winter.

I always have a strong sense that my garden is resting on the cold, grey days of winter. It's a peaceful feeling, and even walking up and down its wintry paths under bare-branched trees is very calming.

The passage of writing that I read that night seemed to encapsulate this perfectly, but instead of applying to my garden, it applied to me and my situation. It encouraged me to think that one of winter's blessings is to remind us to slow down and be kind to ourselves and to renew ourselves and our spirits after a long, hard year.

Life has its sleep, its periods of inactivity, when it loses its movements, takes no new food, living upon its past storage. Then it grows helpless, its muscles relaxed, and it easily lends itself to be jeered at for its stupor.

In the rhythm of life, pauses there must be for the renewal of life. Life in its activity is ever spending itself, burning all its fuel.

This extravagance cannot go on indefinitely, but is always followed by a passive stage, when all expenditure is stopped and all adventures abandoned in favour of rest and slow recuperation.

Rabindranath Tagore

If we had no winter, the spring would not be so pleasant: if we did not sometimes taste of adversity, prosperity would not be so welcome.

Anne Bradstreet

I prefer winter and fall, when you feel the bone structure of the landscape — the loneliness of it — the dead feeling of winter. Something waits beneath it — the whole story doesn't show.

Andrew Wyeth

In my selection of poems, winter in its many states is reflected. From the no-nonsense, matter-of-fact verse of Shakespeare, who tells it exactly as it is, to the pragmatic observations of Longfellow. The magical exuberance of some of the poems for children are a complete contrast to the stark lyrics of Christina Rossetti, whose 'In the Bleak Mid-Winter' has become one of the world's best-loved Christmas carols.

Shakespeare's popular poem 'Winter' makes me shiver. It's so evocative and colourful, and captures every aspect of winter, from the icicles and frozen milk to the coughing and red noses that are part and parcel of the season. Even though it was written around four hundred years ago, it makes me feel that I am part of the same wintry scene.

WINTER

William Shakespeare

When icicles hang by the wall,
And Dick the shepherd blows his nail,
And Tom bears logs into the hall,
And milk comes frozen home in pail,
When blood is nipp'd and ways be foul,
Then nightly sings the staring owl,
Tu-whit Tu-who, a merry note,
While greasy Joan doth keel the pot.

When all aloud the wind doth blow,
And coughing drowns the parson's saw,
And birds sit brooding in the snow,
And Marian's nose looks red and raw,

When roasted crabs hiss in the bowl,
Then nightly sings the staring owl,
Tu-whit Tu-who, a merry note,
While greasy Joan doth keel the pot.

The greatest achievement is selflessness.
The greatest worth is self-mastery.
The greatest quality is seeking to serve others.
The greatest precept is continual awareness.
The greatest medicine is the emptiness of everything.
The greatest action is not conforming with the world's ways.
The greatest magic is transmuting the passions.
The greatest generosity is non-attachment.
The greatest goodness is a peaceful mind.
The greatest patience is humility.
The greatest effort is not concerned with results.
The greatest meditation is a mind that lets go.
The greatest wisdom is seeing through appearances.

Atisha
Buddhist blessing

LONDON SNOW

Robert Bridges

When men were all asleep the snow came flying,
In large white flakes falling on the city brown,
Stealthily and perpetually settling and loosely lying,
Hushing the latest traffic of the drowsy town;
Deadening, muffling, stifling its murmurs failing;
Lazily and incessantly floating down and down:
Silently sifting and veiling road, roof and railing;
Hiding difference, making unevenness even,
Into angles and crevices softly drifting and sailing.
All night it fell, and when full inches seven
It lay in the depth of its uncompacted lightness,
The clouds blew off from a high and frosty heaven;
And all woke earlier for the unaccustomed brightness
Of the winter dawning, the strange unheavenly glare:
The eye marvelled – marvelled at the dazzling
    whiteness;
The ear hearkened to the stillness of the solemn air;
No sound of wheel rumbling nor of foot falling,
And the busy morning cries came thin and spare.
Then boys I heard, as they went to school, calling,
They gathered up the crystal manna to freeze
Their tongues with tasting, their hands with
    snowballing;
Or rioted in a drift, plunging up to the knees;
Or peering up from under the white-mossed wonder,
'O look at the trees!' they cried, 'O look at the trees!'

With lessened load a few carts creak and blunder,
Following along the white deserted way,
A country company long dispersed asunder:
When now already the sun, in pale display
Standing by Paul's high dome, spread forth below
His sparkling beams, and awoke the stir of the day.
For now doors open, and war is waged with the snow;
And trains of sombre men, past tale of number,
Tread long brown paths, as toward their toil they go:
But even for them awhile no cares encumber
Their minds diverted; the daily word is unspoken,
The daily thoughts of labour and sorrow slumber
At the sight of the beauty that greets them, for the
    charm they have broken.

'London Snow' reminds me of childhood, waking up
on a snowy dark morning and seeing a wonderland
outside – the world transformed into a magical,
untouched landscape, so silent and still. But when the
initial sense of delight had worn off I'd wish heartily
that I could stay in bed and not have to go to school,
slipping and sliding on icy paths at the mercy of
snowball-throwing boys, who delighted in tormenting
passers-by with their frozen missiles.

SOUNDS OF THE WINTER

Walt Whitman

Sounds of the winter too,
Sunshine upon the mountains – many a distant strain
From cheery railroad train – from nearer field, barn,
   house,
The whispering air – even the mute crops, garner'd
   apples, corn,
Children's and women's tones – rhythm of many a
   farmer and of flail,
An old man's garrulous lips among the rest, *Think not we
   give out yet*,
Forth from these snowy hairs we keep up yet the lilt.

I love Walt Whitman's phrase 'The whispering air'
in this poem. He conjures up every sound of winter
that you can hear if you stand in a quiet, country
place and just listen. It reminds me of my little haven
in Wicklow, where the sounds of nature do not have
to compete with the roar and bustle of the city.

*Winter is the time for comfort, for good food and warmth,
for the touch of a friendly hand and for a talk
beside the fire: it is the time for home.*

Dame Edith Sitwell

CHILDHOOD WINTER

Children love winter, and never more so than when it snows. To a child, winter is a wondrous season, and snow a source of joy and entertainment, whereas we as adults are conscious of how cold it is, and get irritated when snow and ice disrupt the traffic. We grumble and moan and don't make time to see the wonders of the season, the magical tracery of glistening frost on windows, the pale silvery sheen on lawns and trees or the frozen puddles that invite us to jump on them.

Children see all these glories and more. Maybe if we slowed down and took time to truly look at the beauty of a winter's morning, our spirits would connect to that place of innocence and joy. There is a part of us that connects us to the Divine, which in the frantic pace of modern life we sometimes overlook. Children tap into that place with ease. I've tried to look at the world as they look at it and enjoy their views and perceptions, which bring such freshness, eagerness and delight to every new experience.

Remember as a child how magical it was to wake up, look out of the window and see everywhere covered in white, shining snow? Stripped trees and shrubs had a fresh, crisp dressing. And the pristine lawns called for footprints to dance across the pure, unblemished surface.

My father lived on an island when he was a child. It was called Oyster Island, off Rosses Point in Sligo. His father was a lighthouse keeper. As children, we loved to hear the story of how, one winter, the island was covered in snow. We listened in delight as our father described how he and our aunts and uncles spent hours tobogganing down a hill under a silvery moon and star-studded skies.

They were blue with the cold when they were called in to go to bed. In days when there was no central heating or electric blankets, heated bricks from the oven were placed in the beds, which made them as warm as toast.

We were enthralled with this story and begged him to tell it to us over and over again, and even to this day the grandchildren love to hear it. As a child, I longed to toboggan down a hill in the moonlight and have a bed warmed by bricks, but could only imagine the thrill of it.

Some things never change, though, and snowballs and snowmen are a magical part of winter. These poems describe beautifully the childhood magic of the season and bring back memories of frosty breath turning white, of ruddy cheeks and freezing fingers.

There is always one moment in childhood when the door opens and lets the future in.

Deepak Chopra

One kind word can warm three winter months.

Japanese proverb

SNOWBALL

Shel Silverstein

I made myself a snowball as perfect as could be.
I thought I'd keep it as a pet and let it sleep with me.
I made it some pajamas and a pillow for its head.
Then, last night it ran away.
But first – it wet the bed.

WHITE FIELDS

James Stephens

In winter-time we go
Walking in the fields of snow;
Where there is no grass at all;
Where the top of every wall,
Every fence and every tree,
Is as white as white can be.
Pointing out the way we came –
Every one of them the same –
All across the fields there be
Prints in silver filigree
And our mothers always know
By the footprints in the snow,
Where it is the children go.

WINTER TIME

Robert Louis Stevenson

Late lies the wintry sun a-bed,
A frosty, fiery sleepy-head;
Blinks but an hour or two; and then,
A blood-red orange, sets again.

Before the stars have left the skies,
At morning in the dark I rise;
And shivering in my nakedness,
By the cold candle, bathe and dress.

Close by the jolly fire I sit
To warm my frozen bones a bit;
Or with a reindeer-sled, explore
The colder countries round the door.

When to go out, my nurse doth wrap
Me in my comforter and cap;
The cold wind burns my face, and blows
Its frosty pepper up my nose.

Black are my steps on silver sod;
Thick blows my frosty breath abroad;
And tree and house, and hill and lake,
Are frosted like a wedding cake.

SILVER

Walter de la Mare

Slowly, silently, now the moon
Walks the night in her silver shoon;
This way, and that, she peers, and sees
Silver fruit upon silver trees;
One by one the casements catch
Her beams beneath the silvery thatch;
couched in his kennel, like a log,
with paws of silver sleeps the dog;
From their shadowy cote the white
   breasts peep
Of doves in a silver-feathered sleep;
A harvest mouse goes scampering by,
with silver claws, and silver eye;
And moveless fish in the water gleam,
By silver reeds in a silver stream.

THE SNOWMAN IN THE YARD

Joyce Kilmer

(for Thomas Augustine Daly)

The Judge's house has a splendid porch, with pillars and
   steps of stone,
And the Judge has a lovely flowering hedge that came
   from across the seas;
In the Hales' garage you could put my house and
   everything I own,
And the Hales have a lawn like an emerald and a row of
   poplar trees.

Now I have only a little house, and only a little lot,
And only a few square yards of lawn, with dandelions
   starred;
But when Winter comes, I have something there
that the Judge and the Hales have not,
And it's better worth having than all their wealth –
it's a snowman in the yard.

The Judge's money brings architects to make his
   mansion fair;
The Hales have seven gardeners to make their roses
   grow;
The Judge can get his trees from Spain and France and
   everywhere,

And raise his orchids under glass in the midst of all the
    snow.

But I have something no architect or gardener ever
    made,
A thing that is shaped by the busy touch of little
    mittened hands:
And the Judge would give up his lonely estate, where
    the level snow is laid
For the tiny house with the trampled yard,
the yard where the snowman stands.

They say that after Adam and Eve were driven away in
    tears
To toil and suffer their life-time through,
because of the sin they sinned,
The Lord made Winter to punish them for half their
    exiled years,
To chill their blood with the snow, and pierce
their flesh with the icy wind.

But we who inherit the primal curse, and labour for our
    bread,
Have yet, thank God, the gift of Home, though Eden's
    gate is barred:
And through the Winter's crystal veil, Love's roses
    blossom red,
For him who lives in a house that has a snowman in the
    yard.

LADY IN WHITE

Eileen Sheehan

Out of contrariness,
out of blackguarding,
out of the need
for a small rebellion,
myself and my daughter
built a snow-woman.

Outside of the house
out of clumped snow
we fashioned her –
a sexy dame with a jaunty hat,
big bellied and laughing.

Then we were laughing too
and pleased to meet her
and she not at all surprised
that we'd conjured her to appear,
for one night only,
in our small town-garden.

Meanwhile word had spread
and women from the neighbourhood
were gathering, leading
small girls by the hand. The child
from up the street squirmed
through the laughter to present
her own string of shiny beads.

The man from next-door
couldn't help but give a sideways grin
at the sight of madam in her finery.

And as for herself she just stood there,
coquettishly tilting her head
and taking it all as her due.

But later, as myself and my daughter
held our aching hands to the fire,
she remained, looking
in through the window,
splitting her sides, growing thinner.

By morning she had disappeared
like we knew she would:
snow being the wrong medium;
too slight, too cold to hold her.

Until all around us from
the grass, the garden wall, the roof tops,
the bare trees, the very air,
there exhaled a kind of glistening.

What fire could ever equal the sunshine of a winter's day?

Henry David Thoreau

WINTER GARDEN

The harshness of winter, the short days and long, dark nights can depress and weaken the spirit. We're susceptible to colds and flu and we long to feel heat and warmth in our bones and sunlight on our faces.

But, as always, nature is our ally and there is much to see, enjoy and lift our spirits in our winter garden.

I have a beautiful garden. I love and value my plants hugely and they give me great pleasure. I know some people think it's eccentric, but I love talking to my flowers and shrubs and telling them how wonderful and beautiful they are. I always kiss my camellias when they bloom; they are so gloriously rich and exuberant and such a delightful herald of spring.

I have rich, orange-berried pyracantha, which the birds feast on, and verdant skimmias, which give lovely contrast and colour against the bark of my damson trees. I plant bachelor's buttons – which remind me of fluffy little marshmallows – underneath them. The glorious purples of winter heathers lift the heart and my pots are full of colourful polyanthus and pansies.

I see these beautiful winter blessings as gifts from God, living manifestations of the magnificence of His creation. Even on a wild, windy day, a walk up and down the garden never fails to lift my spirits. I give thanks for all that I've been given and for the beauty that's mine to look upon.

A friend of mine who is an angel therapist told me that a lovely thing to do is to burn incense among the plants and shrubs and invoke the angels to come and fill the garden with their love. It's a very calming, nurturing thing to do and a sense of great peace always envelops me when I do this.

Of course, many people don't have outdoor gardens or don't have the time to take care of the one they have. But even to buy an azalea, a hyacinth or a glorious red and green poinsettia, and care for it and nurture it, brings us close to nature and to the powerful, living energy of the universe.

It's wonderful in the early days in January, when the evenings are getting longer, to see the daffodils and snowdrops thrusting up out of the dark, loamy earth and to see the buds beginning to appear on trees and shrubs. One of the winter garden's greatest gifts, whether indoors or outdoors, is the sense of renewal and new beginnings that we can all share every year, along with the joy and hope this brings.

These poems give a flavour of the darkness and weariness that forms part of winter's richness, but in Laurie Lee's poem there is a reassuring sense of rebirth.

NOVEMBER

Sarah Teasdale

The world is tired, the year is old,
The little leaves are glad to die,
The wind goes shivering with cold
Among the rushes dry.

Our love is dying like the grass,
And we who kissed grow coldly kind,
Half glad to see our poor love pass
Like leaves along the wind.

May your neighbours respect you,
Trouble neglect you,
The angels protect you,
And heaven accept you.

Irish blessing

WINTER POEM

Laurie Lee

Tonight the wind gnaws with teeth of glass
The jackdaw shivers in caged branches of
   iron
The stars have talons
There is hunger in the mouth of vole and
   badger
Silver agonies of breath in the nostril of the
   fox
Ice on the rabbit's paw
Tonight has no moon, no food for the
   pilgrim
The fruit tree is bare, the rose bush a thorn
And the ground is bitter with stones
But the mole sleeps and the hedgehog lies
   curled in a womb of leaves
And the bean and the wheat seed hug their
   germs in the earth
And a stream moves under the ice
Tonight there is no moon
But a star opens like a trumpet over the dead
And tonight in a nest of ruins the blessed
   babe is laid
And the fir tree warms to a bloom of candles
And the child lights his lantern and stares at
   his tinsel toy

And our hearts and hearths smoulder with
    live ashes
In the blood of our grief the cold earth is
    suckled
In our agony the womb convulses its seed
And in the last cry of anguish
The child's first breath is born

THE WARM AND THE COLD

Ted Hughes

Freezing dusk is closing
Like a slow trap of steel
On trees and roads and hills and all
That can no longer feel.
But the carp is in its depth
Like a planet in its heaven
And the badger in its bedding
Like a loaf in the oven.
And the butterfly in its mummy
Like a viol in its case.
And the owl in its feathers
Like a doll in its lace.

Freezing dusk has tightened
Like a nut screwed tight
On the starry aeroplane
Of the soaring night.
But the trout is in its hole
Like a chuckle in a sleeper.
The hare strays down the highway
Like a root going deeper.
The snail is dry in the outhouse
Like a seed in a sunflower.
The owl is pale on the gatepost
Like a clock on its tower.

Moonlight freezes the shaggy world
Like a mammoth of ice –
The past and the future
Are the jaws of a steel vice
But the cod is in the tide-rip
Like a key in a purse.
The deer are on the bare-blown hill
Like smiles on a nurse.
The flies are behind the plaster
Like the lost score of a jig.
Sparrows are in the ivy-clump
Like money in a pig.

Such a frost
The flimsy moon
Has lost her wits.

A star falls.

The sweating farmers
Turn in their sleep
Like oxen on spits.

I love the contrast between Ted Hughes' harsh, cold, outdoors imagery of animals, safe in their havens, and Louis MacNeice's portrayal of the snug, fire-lit, bay-windowed room, where it is easy to imagine the poet pondering life and the universe as he eats a juicy portion of tangerine.

SNOW

Louis MacNeice

The room was suddenly rich and the great
    bay-window was
Spawning snow and pink roses against it
Soundlessly collateral and incompatible:
World is suddener than we fancy it.

World is crazier and more of it than we
    think,
Incorrigibly plural. I peel and portion
A tangerine and spit the pips and feel
The drunkenness of things being various.

And the fire flames with a bubbling sound
    for world
Is more spiteful and gay than one supposes?
On the tongue on the eyes on the ears in the
    palms of one's hands?
There is more than glass between the snow
    and the huge roses.

May you have warm words on a cold evening,
A full moon on a dark night,
And the road downhill all the way to your door.

Irish blessing

Four dry logs have in them all the circumstances necessary to a conversation for four or five hours. Let us love winter, for it is the spring of genius.

Unknown

THE WINTER WALK

One of my great childhood memories is of my parents taking us for long, invigorating walks on Dollymount Strand, a beautiful stretch of beach that is one of Dublin's most famous landmarks. It's part of Bull Island, which also contains one of Europe's best-known wildlife reserves. Birds of all types migrate to feed on its lush, rich ground.

Dollymount's sands are washed by the Irish Sea, and the strand is separated from the wildlife reserve by rolling sand dunes and marram grass. It is a child's paradise. We walked its length through all the seasons and each had its special delights. But for me winter was the best time. Wrapped up in gloves, hats and scarves, we'd tumble out of the car into the wild, bracing wind that swirled and swooped between the dunes. Often we would walk along the strand for the journey out and then come back in the shelter of the dunes, watching the rabbits and hares scamper along, always just out of reach. Sometimes the wind would be so strong we would have to push into it, and the roar of the sea so loud we would have to shout to be heard. Great banks of cloud would threaten rain or even snow. One of the best walks I remember was one St Stephen's Day when it had snowed. The beach was frosted white and the dunes were covered in snow. Snowflakes danced around us, melting into the sea. We felt like Eskimos.

Other days the sky would be cobalt blue, and the sea flat calm, shimmering in the pale, buttery sun. In the distance, Howth rose emerald-green out of the turquoise sea. Brightly coloured kites soaring in the clear skies added to the kaleidoscope of colour.

All this natural beauty was only a fifteen-minute drive away for us and we really made the most of it during our childhood. What games the six of us would play — great adventures that stretched our imaginations and reddened our cheeks and noses in the gusty, spray-speckled wind. We were spies, we were escaped prisoners, we were wild-game hunters or — my favourite — we were cowboys and Indians!

It was a St Stephen's Day tradition in our family to go for a walk on Bull Island. My parents liked us to get fresh air and exercise and often we would moan, wanting to stay at home to play with the toys Santa had brought us.

'Come on, lads, you'll enjoy it when we get there,' my dad would encourage us, as my mother made sure we all had our mittens and scarves to keep us warm. We were so lucky to have such wonderful parents who invested in us the most precious commodity any parent can give a child — their time. As an adult, looking back, I can see how much easier it would have been for them to give in to us. Having worked so hard to prepare for Christmas, and having been up at all hours with the excitement of Santa, they were tired. Much nicer for them to flop after dinner and have a snooze in front of the fire instead of getting us all ready to go out on a cold, often gloomy day.

But my dad was right. We always thoroughly enjoyed ourselves, and, as dusk darkened the skies and grey clouds of night crept inexorably across the Dublin Mountains to the south, we raced back to the car, knowing that a warm fire and tea awaited us, along with our Santa treasures.

Now, when I walk the winter beach on St Stephen's Day, those happy memories warm me. My sister and I have kept up the tradition, although sometimes we compromise and walk along the Bull Wall that stretches out to sea, at the end of which is a massive statue of Our Lady that was erected to protect all seafarers.

Every year we have the same conversation.

'Will we go for a walk?'

'I don't know. What do you want to do?'

'I asked you first.'

'You decide.'

'No, you decide.'

'It's not very nice out.'

'We'd feel better if we went. The girls would get some fresh air.'

'Oh, all right then,' one of us will say grudgingly.

And we always *do* feel exhilarated, even self-righteous, after our brisk walk that has saved us from lolling in front of the TV. My two nieces love it. They dance along ahead of us, screeching and laughing when the waves send mists of spray like fine squirts of perfume over us. Sometimes there are swimmers in the sea and we marvel at their fortitude. We watch the ships sailing into Dublin Port or out of it, glad that we only have to journey home to a warm fireside.

It is so refreshing and cleansing to breathe in the ionised sea air, relishing its purity. As I walk I breathe deeply, inhaling the new and positive and exhaling the old and negative. It's good to imagine releasing all the gloomy, pessimistic thinking that burdens us and breath in positive, confident, assured thoughts that change our energy and give us more courage to face the year ahead.

An outdoor walk in winter, especially on the shortest, darkest days of December, is a gift to our bodies and minds. It can take as long as you wish, costs nothing and the benefits are immense. *And* you'll sleep like a baby afterwards! In this material world we forget the gifts nature has to offer us. When we are overwhelmed with worries and concerns we overlook the simple things that are there to help us along our path.

Although I might moan and groan at the thought of it, I would never forgo my winter walk. Of all the gifts my parents have given to me, the winter walk is one of the greatest, and it is wonderful to see my nieces getting the same enjoyment out of it as we did as children.

The following poem is well known for being a favourite of President J. F. Kennedy. It's easy to see why. Although simply written, it conveys perfectly the deep burden of responsibilities and commitments that we carry. What could be more inviting than to slip away into the dark woods and turn our backs on the world, and how often have we been tempted to do so? Longfellow's poem, 'The Rainy Day', offers us no such temptation and I love his pragmatism when he says:

> Thy fate is the common fate of all,
> Into each life some rain must fall.

STOPPING BY WOODS ON A SNOWY EVENING

Robert Frost

Whose woods thesc are I think I know.
His house is in the village though;
He will not see me stopping here
To watch his woods fill up with snow.

My little horse must think it queer
To stop without a farmhouse near
Between the woods and frozen lake
The darkest evening of the year.

He gives his harness bells a shake
To ask if there is some mistake.
The only other sound's the sweep
Of easy wind and downy flake.

The woods are lovely, dark and deep.
But I have promises to keep,
And miles to go before I sleep,
And miles to go before I sleep.

THE RAINY DAY

Henry Wadsworth Longfellow

The day is cold, and dark, and dreary;
It rains, and the wind is never weary;
The vine still clings to the mouldering wall,
But at every gust the dead leaves fall,
And the day is dark and dreary.

My life is cold, and dark, and dreary;
It rains, and the wind is never weary;
My thoughts still cling to the mouldering Past,
But the hopes of youth fall thick in the blast,
And the days are dark and dreary.

Be still, sad heart! and cease repining;
Behind the clouds is the sun still shining;
Thy fate is the common fate of all,
Into each life some rain must fall,
Some days must be dark and dreary.

WEATHERS

Thomas Hardy

This is the weather the cuckoo likes,
And so do I;
When showers betumble the chestnut spikes,
And nestlings fly:
And the little brown nightingale bills his best,
And they sit outside at 'The Travellers' Rest',
And maids come forth sprig-muslin drest,
And citizens dream of the south and west,
And so do I.

This is the weather the shepherd shuns,
And so do I;
When beeches drip in browns and duns,
And thresh, and ply;
And hill-hid tides throb, throe on throe,
And meadow rivulets overflow,
And drops on gate-bars hang in a row,
And rooks in families homeward go,
And so do I.

Hardy's jaunty, flowery poem is great to read in the middle of winter. We've long forgotten what spring was like and can completely identify with dripping beeches. In contrast, I never fail to be moved by the Christina Rossetti poem, 'In the Bleak Mid-Winter', which is also a beautiful Christmas carol. It is a stark picture of winter, but she reminds us that one of our greatest blessings was the birth of Jesus in a stable in deepest winter.

IN THE BLEAK MID-WINTER

Christina Rossetti

In the bleak mid-winter
Frosty wind made moan;
Earth stood hard as iron,
Water like a stone;
Snow had fallen, snow on snow,
Snow on snow,
In the bleak mid-winter
Long ago.

Our God, heaven cannot hold him
Nor earth sustain;
Heaven and earth shall flee away
When he comes to reign:
In the bleak mid-winter
A stable place sufficed
The Lord God Almighty,
Jesus Christ.

Enough for Him, Whom cherubim,
Worship night and day,
Breastful of milk,
And a mangerful of hay;
Enough for Him,
Whom angels fall before,
The ox and ass and camel
Which adore.

Angels and archangels
May have gathered there,
Cherubim and seraphim
Thronged the air;
But His mother only,
In her maiden bliss,
Worshipped the beloved
With a kiss.

What can I give Him,
Poor as I am?
If I were a shepherd,
I would bring a lamb;
If I were a Wise Man,
I would do my part;
Yet what I can I give Him:
Give my heart.

Part Two
CHRISTMAS

May peace and
plenty be the first
To lift the latch to your door,
And happiness be guided to your home
By the candle of Christmas.

Irish blessing

THE ART OF GIVING
AND RECEIVING

Another of winter's blessings that breaks the short, gloomy days and long, cold nights is the celebration of Christmas. In the run-up to Christmas much of our time is taken up with buying gifts for loved ones. To many, this is a source of joy; to many more, a chore. There is much talk about how commercial the season has become, how material considerations have overtaken the spiritual side of the celebration of Christ's birth. But when I see the shops thronged with shoppers, fraught and harassed, buying gifts for family and friends, I see love.

How often have we spent ages dithering over this gift or the other for a dear one? Which will give the most pleasure? Can there be anything better than finding the perfect gift? It has nothing to do with cost and size and all to do with finding a gift that will give joy.

A dear friend of mine spent weeks looking for a kettle that would not trip the electricity switch in my mobile home where I spend a lot of time during the summer. He searched high and low all over Dublin and triumphantly produced it on Christmas Eve. I'm now the envy of friends and family whose switches trip frequently, and have promised to lend it to them when they're entertaining.

Another very dear friend bought me long-handled clippers so that I wouldn't have to bend when I was edging the grass, as he knew how painful it was for me to garden because of my back problems. It was the perfect present.

These gifts, and many more that I've received, have been given with love and thoughtful kindness and have left me quite overwhelmed.

For some of us, it can be harder to receive a gift than to give one. We feel unworthy, guilty even, that someone has gone to such trouble for us.

I was once told by a very wise friend that I must learn to feel worthy of the gifts I receive. Recently my sister and brother-in-law gave me a present of a flight to Spain. I protested and said it was too much and that there was no need for them to be so generous. 'I thought you were supposed to be learning the art of receiving gracefully,' my much-loved straight-talking sister said. 'You're not doing a very good job of it, if I may say so.'

I burst out laughing and had to admit that she was right. The more we open up to receive, the more the abundance of the universe will pour down upon us. The more we acknowledge our worthiness to receive, the greater the gifts will be. Jesus said we must love our neighbours as *ourselves*. Often, loving ourselves is the hardest thing in the world to do. In receiving gifts we are opening up to an act of love from another. By allowing ourselves to receive, we allow the other to give, and both the giver and the receiver are then doubly blessed.

In her book, *The Game of Life and How to Play It*, Florence Scovel-Shinn says that 'God is the Giver and the Gift' and she gives us the wonderful prayer: *'I now thank God the Giver for God the Gift.'* When we think of giving and receiving gifts in this way it makes it a much more powerful and spiritual act and so becomes easier to receive gracefully our abundance from the universe.

Often at Christmas people feel they have to buy presents for people they don't really care for. The in-laws they don't get on with, the crotchety aunt or uncle, the neighbour who gets up their nose. But they know that not to buy something, no matter how small it is, will cause offence or hurt.

Many would consider this kind of gift-buying hypocritical. But in the buying of that gift there *is* a loving act in not deliberately hurting someone by withholding it. While human love might not be there, soul love is, and we should acknowledge that in ourselves rather than focusing on feelings of guilt or hypocrisy.

It's not possible to love or even like everyone,

nor are we obliged to, as long as we recognise the divinity and equality of each soul and reflect that in our treatment of others.

I remember every year as a child getting high-heeled Cinderella slippers for Christmas. These gave me the greatest delight. I felt so grown up clip-clopping along in them. My mother went to a lot of trouble to get them as they were like gold dust. She would traipse from Grafton Street to Henry Street in the search for the 'Cinderella High Heels' that were invariably requested in my letter to Santa. My parents went to the ends of the earth to get presents for the six of us that we would all enjoy. I remember magnificent train sets, pearl-handled cowboy guns, china dolls and rocking-horses, to name but a few. In those days we had no car and they had to be lugged home on the bus and hidden in our neighbour's attic.

The memory of that love comes back every Christmas and I see now how my own sister and brothers go to the ends of the earth for their children. Love was shown to us, and we in turn now show love to our precious darlings. They are learning, as we did, that the art of giving and receiving is love and love is what it's all about ultimately: the greatest gift of all.

CHRISTMAS PRESENTS

Anon

Every year Grandma gets a tin of talcum powder.
She always says, 'Ah my favourite!'
Even before she opens the wrapping.
Grandpa always says, 'Well, I know what's in here.
It's two pairs of socks. Just what I wanted!'

This year, Aunti Vi had an umbrella in an umbrella-
    shaped parcel,
I mean, it looked just like an umbrella.
And, before Aunti Vi pulled the paper off,
She said to Mum, 'It will match that new coat of
    mine.'

As for Mum and Dad, they just sat there and said,
'We've given each other a joint present this year
It's a digital clock radio for our bedroom.'
Do you know, they didn't even bother to wrap it
    up and put it under the tree?

At the end, when everything had been given out,
Mum said, 'We mustn't forget the gift-vouchers
    from Debbie and Jim.
We sent them a cheque for the same amount.
We always do.'
I call that a bit unimaginative, don't you?

Maybe, when you come to think about it,
Grown-ups need Father Christmas far more than
children do.

*You can explore the universe looking for somebody who is
more deserving of your love and affection than you are
yourself, and you will not find that person anywhere.*

Buddha

People don't notice whether it's winter or summer when they're happy.

Anton Chekhov

Happiness does not come from having much, but from being attached to little.

Unknown

A WINTER NIGHT

Sara Teasdale

My window-pane is starred with frost,
The world is bitter cold to-night,
The moon is cruel and the wind
Is like a two-edged sword to smite.

God pity all the homeless ones,
The beggars pacing to and fro.
God pity all the poor to-night
Who walk the lamp-lit streets of snow.

My room is like a bit of June,
Warm and close-curtained fold on fold,
But somewhere, like a homeless child,
My heart is crying in the cold.

God is day and night, winter and summer, war and peace, surfeit and hunger.

Heraclitus of Ephesus

LOSS

For many people, Christmas can be a desperately sad and lonely time. At no time does the pain of loss feel more intense and poignant. At no other time does the sense of aloneness and loneliness seem so daunting, particularly for people who are on their own. A friend of mine, who finds Christmas difficult, decided last year to help out serving dinners to the homeless. It was, she said, one of the best Christmas

Days she'd ever had. By reaching out, instead of looking inward, her own spirit was nurtured and she felt she received far more than she gave. She told me that she'll never again dread Christmas Day the way she used to.

For those touched by bereavement, the sadness is always intensified at Christmas time. The present that no longer has to be bought, the card that's no longer sent or received, emphasise the sense of loss. The loved one, no longer there to share, leaves an ache that is almost unbearable.

A few years ago my sister's mother-in-law died. Coming up to Christmas the family went to visit her grave. My niece, who had only started school that September, went straight to the headstone and hugged it. 'Hello Granny,' she said, very matter-of-factly. She turned to my sister and asked, 'Mom, do you think Granny would like to see the Irish dancing I learned at school?'

'I think she'd be delighted,' my sister replied, touched by her innocence and knowing that her mother-in-law, who had a lively sense of humour, would have been hugely entertained. There and then, upon her granny's grave, my niece danced her heart out, joyfully and exuberantly, supremely confident that her granny could see and hear her.

I wonder, would the loss of bereavement become more bearable if only we could regain that innocent trust and become like children again? I watched an interview with a man who lost his wife to the tsunami that struck on the day after Christmas. He and his four children survived. He spoke of how his young children seemed to be coping with the loss of their mother far better than he was. The youngest left notes in the window and waved up at the sky often, certain that her mother could see her.

Jesus said, '*Let the little children come to me, and do not hinder them, for the kingdom of heaven belongs to such as these.*' (Matthew xix, 14). He knew that the innocence and trust displayed by children is the way to have spiritual knowledge. If, like my niece, we could have the trust to know that our loved ones are as near to us as we want them to be, how much less painful the loss would be.

I find it very comforting to imagine Jesus in His human form, knowing that He too lived through all that we experience. He too suffered the pain of loss and wept when told of the death of his dear friend,

Lazarus. Those who saw this said, '*See how much He loved him!*' (John xi, 36). Jesus understands completely our grief and sorrow, and we are told: *Happy those who mourn; They shall be comforted.* (Matthew v, 4)

And there *is* comfort there for us if we are open to it. All the great masters, from Buddha to Muhammad to Jesus, tell us this. We don't have to practise any particular religion to agree with the truth of these words. My niece brought great comfort with her innocent, heartfelt gift of dance and trust, and what at that age would she know of religion? But she knows all about love and trust.

I do not believe at all that you have to be very 'religious' in the traditional sense of the word to have a spiritual dimension to your life. Although I speak of my profound belief in and love of Jesus, and of the way He has helped me on my path, I certainly would not describe myself as 'religious'. But in my experiences of loss – loss of loved ones through death, loss in relationships, loss of my physical fitness – I have been sustained and comforted by Him. He has seen the worst of me and the best of me and still accepts me, and isn't that what the perfect relationship is all about? The relief of being totally yourself with someone you love is a very special gift. Why should it be any different with God or Jesus, or Buddha or Muhammad, or any Divinity we choose?

A very special friend, who has helped many people on their spiritual journey, once gave me the gift of a most beautiful blessing:

> May the Peace of the Lord be within you.
> May the Grace of the Lord surround you.

It's a wonderful blessing to say to yourself or to another, in times of distress or fear. To visualise yourself, or the person you're blessing, surrounded by the powerful white light of grace as you say it, gives a sense of calm and well-being that brings balm to the distressed spirit. As Jesus said to us:

'Peace I bequeath to you; my own peace I give you; a peace the world cannot give, this is my gift to you. Do not let your hearts be troubled or afraid.' (John xiv, 27)

It is very comforting to sit quietly, light a candle and play some soothing music to help quieten your thoughts. Next, visualise your departed loved one happy and peaceful, and free of all illness, stress and worry, in a beautiful place. Often, when I do this, I feel enveloped by a sense of peace, and find the strength to move on.

Do not pursue the past.
Do not lose yourself in the future.
The past no longer is.
The future has not yet come.
Looking deeply at life as it is.
In the very here and now, the
  practitioner dwells in stability and
  freedom.
We must be diligent today.
To wait until tomorrow is too late.
Death comes unexpectedly.
How can we bargain with it?
The sage calls a person who knows
  how to dwell in mindfulness night
  and day,
'one who knows the better way to live
  alone.'

Bhaddekaratta Sutta
Buddhist blessing

Grace groweth best in winter.

Samuel Rutherford

WE WON'T HAVE A CHRISTMAS THIS YEAR

Verna S. Teeuwissen

We won't have a Christmas this year, you say
For now the children have all gone away;
And the house is so lonely, so quiet and so bare
We couldn't have a Christmas that they didn't
    share.

We won't have a Christmas this year, you sigh,
For Christmas means things that money must
    buy.
Misfortunes and illness have robbed us we fear
Of the things that we'd need to make
    Christmas this year.

We won't have a Christmas this year you weep,
For a loved one is gone, and our grief is too
    deep;
It will be a long time before our hearts heal,
And the spirit of Christmas again we can feel.

But if you lose Christmas when troubles befall,
You never have really had Christmas at all.
For once you have had it, it cannot depart
When you learn that true Christmas is Christ
    in your heart.

In Verna S. Teeuwissen's poem, 'We Won't Have a Christmas This Year', the sense of loss is movingly evoked, but so too is the sense of hope and comfort. In the beautiful poem 'Father and Son', by F. R. Higgins, the love of a son for his father is poignant and touching. All the memories of him come back as the son walks along the river bank and comforts himself that there is some of his father in him.

FATHER AND SON

F. R. Higgins

Only last week, walking the hushed fields
Of our most lovely Meath, now thinned by
    November,
I came to where the road from Laracor leads
To the Boyne river – that seems more lake
    than river,
Stretched in uneasy light and stript of reeds.
And walking longside an old weir
Of my people's, where nothing stirs – only the
    shadowed
Leaden flight of a heron up the lean air –
I went unmanly with grief, knowing how my
    father,
Happy though captive in years, walked last
    with me there.

Yes, happy in Meath with me for a day
He walked, taking stock of herds hid in their
    own breathing;
And naming colts, gusty as wind, once steered
    by his hand,
Lightnings winked in the eyes that were half
    shy in greeting
Old friends – the wild blades, when he
    gallivanted the land.

For that proud, wayward man now my heart
   breaks –
Breaks for that man whose mind was a secret
   eyrie,
Whose kind hand was sole signet of his race,
Who curbed me, scorned my green ways, yet
   increasingly loved me
Till Death drew its grey blind down his face.

And yet I am pleased that even my reckless
   ways
Are living shades of his rich calms and passions –
Witnesses for him and for those faint
   namesakes
With whom now he is one, under yew
   branches,
Yes, one in a graven silence no bird breaks.

Never cut a tree down in the winter. Never make a negative decision in the low time. Never make your most important decisions when you are in your worst moods. Wait. Be patient. The storm will pass. The spring will come.

Robert Schuller

Sometimes our fate resembles a fruit tree in winter. Who would think that those branches would turn green again and bloom, but we hope it, we know it.

Johann Wolfgang von Goethe

CHRISTMAS MEMORIES

I love Christmas. For me it's always been a time for family, and if I could go back and live one day of my childhood again I'd choose a Christmas Eve when we were small. I have four brothers and one sister, and my parents made Christmas the most magical time for us.

It all started with the trip to town to see the Christmas lights and gaze in awe at the shop windows. Shop windows didn't have shutters in those days and Dublin was a safer, friendlier city. 'Five for ten the Christmas wrappin' paper!' The cries of the traders in Moore Street, blending with the voices of the carol singers, was a Christmas symphony. The fairy lights laced along Henry Street and North Earl Street, embroidering the trees along O'Connell Street, which sparkled like Weir's window.

The six of us would empty our moneyboxes and have many uproarious meetings as arguments raged about what Christmas presents to buy. Hankies, socks, perfume and bath cubes were some of our favourite choices – no matter what the gift, my parents always looked suitably surprised and delighted. It was only years later that my mother confessed that she hated bath cubes! Woolworths or Roches stores were the best for Christmas shopping.

We'd be in a fever pitch of excitement. Any naughtiness on our part (and there was plenty) was met with the threat, 'Santa's listening!'

By Christmas Eve our excitement knew no bounds as we sat around the kitchen table with the fire roaring up the chimney and my mother making the stuffing. All ears would be tuned to the big old wireless as Santa's helper, Aidan, read out the letters from children around the country. We'd listen, with mounting excitement, as Aidan led us to the countdown to Santa's departure. When the magic words came – 'He's off!' – it was time for baths, tea and bed.

We always had turkey necks for tea on Christmas Eve, with chunky slices of Vienna roll. Those necks were thick and meaty, unlike the scrawny little offerings you get today, if you're lucky.

We'd troop upstairs in a tizzy of anticipation to hang up our Christmas stockings.

'Where is he now, Daddy?'

'Greenland, I'd say, lads. Into bed now, quick.'

I still remember the sight of those limp, grey stockings dangling from the bedposts.

'Now where is he, Daddy?'

'Heading for Iceland now. Hurry on, he'll be here soon.'

Giddy speculation would issue forth between the bedrooms, while downstairs mouthwatering smells wafted from the kitchen.

In those days there was no such thing as putting your tree up weeks in advance. Our crib, tree and decorations went up on Christmas Eve when we were all in bed. My parents worked like Trojans to create a magical wonderland for us.

Exhausted from excitement, we'd drift off to sleep, half-fearful of waking and finding Santa in the room or hearing the reindeer's hooves on the roof.

I can't describe to you the heart-in-mouth experience of waking in the dark to feel a heavy weight on your feet. Has he come? you'd wonder, and give an experimental wiggle. Yes, definitely something heavy at your feet. Happiness, exhilaration and relief that you had been good enough to get a present from Santa.

'He's come, he's come!' someone would shout, and we'd all race into our parents' bedroom, exploring stockings with their treasure trove of satsumas, a white hanky, toffee sweets and a shiny new penny. We'd scamper downstairs and close our eyes until my father plugged in the lights of the Christmas tree. We'd stand in awe and wonder at my father's creation. He took great pride in his tree, and to this day all of us will try to find the fullest, firmest, most perfect tree possible.

My mother's crib was another source of joy and delight. Baby Jesus lay in His manger, with straw on the floor and ivy trailing over the black papier mâché mountains that the Three Wise Men had just traversed. An old silver sheriff's badge atop the crib shone more brightly than any star of Bethlehem. We still have that star and crib and all the figurines, although one of the sheep has lost a leg.

After breakfast we'd troop off to early Mass, freezing breath frosty white, hoping it might snow. The church would be full and the choir was always beautiful. *Everybody* sang the carols loudly and lustily, or so it seemed to me. Even now, all these years on, I still find on Christmas morning the air of innocence, joy and excitement that I remember from my childhood.

The crib in our church in Ballygall was enormous and after Mass we would clamber over one another at the altar rail to get the best view. To a child's eye the large figures of the Holy Family looked almost lifelike. We would be reduced to silence at the mystery and magic of the scene in front of us. This part of Christmas Day was as significant to us as the presents and the tree, and we were lucky that our parents made the spiritual side of Christmas as important and joyful as the material side.

After Mass we would visit family and neighbours before heading home for the dinner. And how special that dinner of turkey and ham and pudding and brandy butter was to the six of us. The excitement of pulling the crackers, the hearty laughter over the silly jokes. The toasting of our parents, 'The best mammy and daddy in the world.' Clinking our glasses filled with grape juice. How grown up we felt we were. And there was even more excitement to come – 'The Presents Under the Tree' ritual. We never opened our presents until after dinner and I remember how long the washing up seemed to take when there was a mountain of presents waiting to be opened. My mother would sit beside the Christmas tree and hand out a present to each of us. It was almost as exciting as Santa's arrival.

We always got a Christmas annual each, *Bunty* or *Judy*, *Dandy* or *Beano*. Weary and full, we'd plonk down in front of the fire and read our annuals under the lights of the tree, with the flames of the fire flickering and dancing along the walls as dusk settled – another magical Christmas Day almost over. And so, after Christmas cake and mince pies, to bed. Six very happy children. We had many such Christmases, and to this day being together as a family at Christmas is one of my greatest joys. This selection of poems brings me back to those happy, carefree days.

THE CHRISTMAS
PUDDING

Anon

Into the basin
put the plums,
Stir-about, stir-about,
stir-about!

Next the good
white flour comes,
Stir-about, stir-about,
stir about!

Sugar and peel
and eggs and spice,
Stir-about, stir-about,
stir-about!

Mix them and fix them
and cook them twice,
Stir-about, stir-about,
stir-about!

FOR THE CHILDREN
OR THE GROWN-UPS

Anon

'Tis the week before Christmas and every
  night
As soon as the children are snuggled up tight
And have sleepily murmured their wishes and
  prayers,
Such fun as goes on in the parlour downstairs!
For Father, Big Brother, and Grandfather too,
Start in with great vigour their youth to renew.
The grown-ups are having great fun – all is
  well;
And they play till it's long past their hour for
  bed.

They try to solve puzzles and each one enjoys
The magical thrill of mechanical toys,
Even Mother must play with a doll that can
  talk,
And if you assist it, it's able to walk.
It's really no matter if paint may be scratched,
Or a cogwheel, a nut, or a bolt gets detached;
The grown-ups are having great fun – all is
  well;
The children don't know it, and Santa won't
  tell.

A CHRISTMAS CANDLE

Lucy Brennan

Last night I left a candle burning
behind the Christ Child in the manger.
I woke at dawn and rushed to quench the light.

Christmas Eve when I had just turned twenty,
my job to light the candle in the window
that overlooked the road, the beach, the sea.
I set it in the bay and drew across
the heavy velvet drapes – its light thrown out
onto the street to welcome homeless travellers –
and went to help my mother stuff the turkey.

At midnight, a knock came on the door.
Startled, our eyes spoke of all wanderers.
A knock, an urgency, a need,
and it was Christmas.
Again the knocking came.
My mother's hands so full of crumbs,
of sage, thyme, onions, parsley,
helplessness: I went.

A man, white-faced, almost speechless; behind –
the street, the dark, the pounding waves, the stars.
'Fire! Your curtains! The candle's fallen over!'

Each year I light a candle for the Christ Child:
I've opened doors so many times since then.

A CHRISTMAS CHILDHOOD

Patrick Kavanagh

1

One side of the potato-pits was white with
   frost —
How wonderful that was, how wonderful!
And when we put our ears to the paling-
   post
The music that came out was magical.

The light between the ricks of hay and straw
Was a hole in Heaven's gable. An apple tree
With its December-glinting fruit we saw —
O you, Eve, were the world that tempted me

To eat the knowledge that grew in clay
And death the germ within it! Now and then
I can remember something of the gay
Garden that was childhood's. Again

The tracks of cattle to a drinking-place,
A green stone lying sideways in a ditch
Or any common sight, the transfigured face
Of a beauty that the world did not touch.

2

My father played the melodion
Outside at our gate;
There were stars in the morning east
And they danced to his music.

Across the wild bogs his melodion called
To Lennons and Callans.
As I pulled on my trousers in a hurry
I knew some strange thing had happened.

Outside the cow-house my mother
Made the music of milking;
The light of her stable-lamp was a star
And the frost of Bethlehem made it twinkle.

A water-hen screeched in the bog,
Mass-going feet
Crunched the wafer-ice on the pot-holes,
Somebody wistfully twisted the bellows wheel.

My child poet picked out the letters
On the grey stone,
In silver the wonder of a Christmas
    townland,
The winking glitter of a frosty dawn.

Cassiopeia was over
Cassidy's hanging hill,
I looked and three whin bushes rode across
The horizon – the Three Wise Kings.

An old man passing said:
'Can't he make it talk? –
The melodion.' I hid in the doorway
And tightened the belt of my box-pleated coat.

I nicked six nicks on the door-post
With my penknife's big blade –
There was a little one for cutting tobacco.
And I was six Christmases of age.

My father played the melodion,
My mother milked the cows,
And I had a prayer like a white rose pinned
On the Virgin Mary's blouse.

Laughter is the sun that drives winter from the human face.

Victor Hugo

THE RECKONING

Anon

Now the festive season's ended
Comes the sequel parents dread;
Pale and visibly distended
Bilious Tommy lies in bed,
Face to face with retribution
And an outraged constitution.

What a change since, pink and perky
Tommy swiftly put away
Three enormous goes of turkey
At the feast on Christmas Day,
Getting by judicious bluffing
Double quantities of stuffing.

As to pudding, who could reckon
Tommy's load in terms of size?
Who attempt to keep a check on
Tommy's numberless mince pies?
Hopeless task! His present pallor
Proves his prodigies of valour.

Then I found him, notwithstanding
Such colossal feats as these,
After dinner on the landing
Secretly devouring cheese,
Flanked by ginger-beer-and-coffee,
Sweetened with a slab of toffee.

I, his uncle, gave him warning,
Showed him the error of his ways,
Hinted at tomorrow morning,
Talked about my boyhood days;
All in vain I waved the bogey
He despised me as a fogey.

Well, perhaps the pains he suffers
May be gifts of fairy gold,
Since he now says, 'Only duffers
Eat as much as they can hold.'
Thus, through physic and privations,
Tommy learns his limitations.

Winter is not a season; it's an occupation.

Sinclair Lewis

At Christmas I no more desire a rose
Than wish a snow in May's new-fangled mirth;
But like of each thing that in season grows.

William Shakespeare, from *Love's Labour's Lost*

WINTRY SEAS

My father and twin brother were seamen. Both of them went 'deep sea' and were away from home for long passages of time. Fortunately, my father became a tug captain in Dublin Port after he married my mother and was never away from home once we were born. My twin brother is now also a tug captain in Dublin and his days of deep-sea voyages are also behind him, much to our relief. When a family member is away from home there's always a little worry at the back of your mind. My mother always listens intently to the weather forecast to this day, to see what's happening from Malin Head to Mizzen Head and beyond. On stormy nights I always say a prayer for sailors, knowing how treacherous and unpredictable the sea can be.

My father and brother told us many hair-raising stories of life on the ocean waves, and it was a life of great adventure. I remember vividly as a child how my father would gather us all round a huge map of the world and point out all the ports he had sailed into – exotic places with names like Rio de Janeiro, Java, Jakarta, Yokohama, La Plata, New York, Penang, Singapore, Manila, Hong Kong. I'd roll those names around my tongue and I delighted in being able to point them out on the map at school. One-upmanship is great when you're a child!

I particularly like the next two poems because they evoke the wild, stormy, wintry seas and the dangers faced by sailors. In 'The Tempest', when all seems lost and all hands are busy praying, a little child says:

> Isn't God upon the ocean,
> Just the same as on the land?

The innocent belief of the child brings calm to her father, the captain, and all the crew. Many are the prayers that are said for seamen, especially in the winter. My mother, who lost a brother at sea during the war, loves this poem.

'Christmas At Sea' by Robert Louis Stevenson also evokes a stormy passage when all seems lost. It tells of how lonely it is for the sailor who can see his home and knows that his parents are talking about him and missing him on Christmas Day.

Our Christmases at home were always tinged with loneliness when my brother was away at sea, especially when we sat down to dinner. It was never quite the same. If we were lucky we would get a ship-to-shore phone call. But saying goodbye would be really sad and there'd be a few sneaky tears. Other years, when we knew that he would be home for Christmas, the excitement and joy was an extra blessing of the whole family being together again.

BALLAD OF THE TEMPEST

James T. Fields

We were crowded in the cabin;
Not a soul would dare to sleep:
It was midnight on the waters,
And a storm was on the deep.

'Tis a fearful thing in winter
To be shattered by the blast,
And to hear the rattling trumpet
Thunder, 'Cut away the mast!'

So we shuddered there in silence,
For the stoutest held his breath,
While the hungry sea was roaring,
And the breakers threatened death.

And as thus we sat in darkness,
Each one busy in his prayers,
'We are lost!' the captain shouted,
As he staggered down the stairs.

But his little daughter whispered,
As she took his icy hand,
'Isn't God upon the ocean,
Just the same as on the land?'

Then we kissed the little maiden,
And we spoke in better cheer;
And we anchored safe in harbor
When the morn was shining clear.

CHRISTMAS AT SEA

Robert Louis Stevenson

The sheets were frozen hard, and they cut the naked
    hand;
The decks were like a slide, where a seaman scarce
    could stand;
The wind was a nor'wester, blowing squally off the sea;
And cliffs and spouting breakers were the only things
    a-lee.

They heard the surf a-roaring before the break of day;
But 'twas only with the peep of light we saw how ill we
    lay.
We tumbled every hand on deck instanter, with a shout,
And we gave her the maintops'l, and stood by to go
    about.

All day we tacked and tacked between the South Head
    and the North;
All day we hauled the frozen sheets, and got no further
    forth;
All day as cold as charity, in bitter pain and dread,
For very life and nature we tacked from head to head.

We gave the South a wider berth, for there the tide-race
    roared;
But every tack we made we brought the North Head
    close aboard:

So's we saw the cliffs and houses, and the breakers
    running high,
And the coastguard in his garden, with his glass against
    his eye.

The frost was on the village roofs as white as ocean
    foam;
The good red fires were burning bright in every
    'longshore home;
The windows sparkled clear, and the chimneys volleyed
    out;
And I vow we sniffed the victuals as the vessel went
    about.

The bells upon the church were rung with a mighty
    jovial cheer;
For it's just that I should tell you how (of all days in the
    year)
This day of our adversity was blessed Christmas morn,
And the house above the coastguard's was the house
    where I was born.

O well I saw the pleasant room, the pleasant faces there,
My mother's silver spectacles, my father's silver hair;
And well I saw the firelight, like a flight of homely elves,
Go dancing round the china-plates that stand upon the
    shelves.

And well I knew the talk they had, the talk that was of me,
Of the shadow on the household and the son that went
    to sea;

And O the wicked fool I seemed, in every kind of way,
To be here and hauling frozen ropes on blessed
    Christmas Day.

They lit the high sea-light, and the dark began to fall.
'All hands to loose topgallant sails,' I heard the captain
    call.
'By the Lord, she'll never stand it,' our first mate,
    Jackson, cried.
… 'It's the one way or the other, Mr. Jackson,' he replied.

She staggered to her bearings, but the sails were new
    and good,
And the ship smelt up to windward just as though she
    understood.
As the winter's day was ending, in the entry of the night,
We cleared the weary headland, and passed below the
    light.

And they heaved a mighty breath, every soul on board
    but me,
As they saw her nose again pointing handsome out to
    sea;
But all that I could think of, in the darkness and the
    cold,
Was just that I was leaving home and my folks were
    growing old.

NEW YEAR ENDINGS
AND BEGINNINGS

New Year's Eve can be a very difficult time for many of us. There's something about it that gives rise to feelings of loss or regret, dissatisfaction or depression. Maybe the previous year hasn't gone so well. Perhaps we feel that we've failed in some way when we look back on what we perceive as a lack of achievement. New Year's Eve can be a lonely night if we don't have that 'someone special' to share it with. Or if the relationship we're in is not working.

New Year's Eve can also be a very positive time, a time of new beginnings and resolutions. A lot depends on the way we look at it and our frame of mind.

I like the old tradition of opening the door to hear the bells ring out and to let the old year out and the new year in.

I used to hate the New Year. In my teens and twenties I frequently felt like a failure. New Year's Eve seemed to magnify these feelings, and although I would go out and party and sing 'Auld Lang Syne', I was always glad when it was over.

One New Year's Eve I was too fed up to leave the house. My first novel, *City Girl*, had been politely rejected by a few publishers that year. Some had taken the trouble to write encouraging comments, but, nevertheless, rejection is rejection. I was beginning to doubt that I would ever be a published writer.

The night dragged on and I became more restless and agitated. Finally I went to my room and muttered to myself, 'For heaven's sake, do something positive.' I sat at my little portable typewriter and typed a letter to a publisher whose name had been given to me by an agent. I explained that I was sending the first three chapters of my first novel. Needless to say, I didn't mention that other publishers had turned it down. I remembered reading in a book on how to get published that it was imperative to keep the letter short but say something that would catch the publisher's attention so the manuscript wouldn't be sent to languish on the slush pile. I assured him that he if he published *City Girl* he would become a millionaire. I signed the letter, put it in an envelope and addressed it. All my negativity evaporated through the very act of doing something positive, and I enjoyed the rest of the night – all my optimism returned.

Being positive that night certainly worked; indeed, it was a turning point in my life. I posted the letter on the first of January and three days later I received a phone call from an editor who wanted to read the rest of the manuscript and meet me. Two weeks later I signed my first contract and received the princely advance of £150.

It was a great lesson in positive thinking and I have never dreaded New Year's Eve again. Now I always do one positive thing, whether it's filling a black sack with clutter, dealing with a task I've kept putting off or even just lighting a candle and asking for all negativity to leave me so that I can be filled with positive energy.

Cutting the ties with any negative things from the passing year is a very useful thing to do on New Year's Eve. It could be a difficult situation or a difficult relationship that has troubled you. It's very simple to light your candle and pray to whomever you wish to come and help you. Next, visualise the situation or person being released from you and you from them, to leave through your front door with the old year so that difficulties can end and new beginnings can take place. If there is an unresolved situation in your life, ask the universe for the right outcome to happen.

If you feel oppressed by a particularly dark energy, call upon St Michael to cut the ties with the difficulty you are facing so that you are no longer bound by the oppression. Visualise light around yourself, or around the person or situation that is troubling you. As it leaves your house, let go with a blessing. You will feel such relief and be able to deal with your problems in a much more positive way.

Blessing a person or situation that has brought you difficulties is a wonderful way of taking back your own power. Letting go of negative thoughts, anger and resentment is a powerful exercise that will fill you with a new energy and change your thinking for ever. Your mind will become clearer and the decisions you make will come easier to you.

Angry, resentful and bitter thoughts eat up a person. Letting go is the most liberating, life-enhancing choice anyone can make. A person who lets go will reap the benefits almost instantly.

The next step in the process of cutting the ties is to ask for the 'right outcome' or for the 'right person' to come into your life.

New Year's Eve is a powerful time to make new decisions for the better. We always have choices in life, though we don't always recognise it. We make choices in what we think, whether the focus of our thoughts is positive or negative. Once we change our way of thinking for the better, and no longer allow ourselves to be consumed by negativity, bad situations can change and sometimes even fade away.

If you are in the happy position of having no unhappy memories or situations to do away with, it's lovely to just open the door and welcome in the New Year, asking for your life to be filled with whatever joyful, positive things you wish for.

'*Ask and you shall receive,*' we are told. Many doors opened to me when I asked with faith. And they are opening all the time. By surrendering and releasing difficult situations, we allow a greater power to direct our path and the burden is taken from us, leaving us free to enjoy the gifts that have been given to us.

The object of a new year is not that we should have a new year. It is that we should have a new soul.

G. K. Chesterton

New Year's Eve is like every other night: there is no pause in the march of the universe, no breathless moment of silence among created things that the passage of another twelve months may be noted; and yet no man has quite the same thoughts this evening that come with the coming of darkness on other nights.

Hamilton Wright Mabie

If there is a God, we're all it.

John Lennon

Part Three

HOPE AND RENEWAL

Thousands of candles can be lit from a single candle,
and the life of the candle will not be shortened.
Happiness never decreases by being shared.

Buddha

THE ANGELS OF WINTER

Every season is under the protection of its own angels and the Angels of Winter take care of the earth as it settles down to rest and renew itself in the dark days of that season. In November, I always hand over my garden to the protection of the angels and light an incense stick to welcome them. Ever since I started doing this, the plants and flowers seem to be thriving, blossoming more luxuriantly than ever, and the garden has become even more of a haven, with a beautiful feeling of serenity flowing through it. Even my indoor plants – hyacinths, pyracantha and azaleas – bloom for so much longer when I ask the angels to bless them.

St Michael, the Angel of the North and the Angel of Protection, is the one I turn to in my hour of need. This mighty archangel is a powerful protector. I started praying to him for his protection many years ago and he has never let me down. As children we used to say that most beautiful of prayers, the Prayer to our Guardian Angel.

> Oh angel of God my guardian dear,
> To whom God's love commits me here,
> Ever this day be at my side,
> To light and guard, to rule and guide,
> Amen.

It's a powerful prayer and, even to this day, when I say it I feel comforted. Just saying that little prayer in the morning raises my energy to a spiritual level and I know that whatever cares or concerns the day brings I will not be carrying them alone.

St Michael can infuse you with courage. When I was having difficulties in my professional life, and seemed threatened with legal problems I was very apprehensive. I completely lost the ability to write and was petrified that I would never write again. A dear friend gave me a statue of St Michael and told me to pray to him and ask for his protection and help. I placed the small statue beside the fax machine, where the solicitor's letters that would tie up my stomach in knots arrived. 'Please, please, help me, I'm afraid,' I pleaded in despair.

From then on I never felt as beleaguered. I was even able to free up my mind from fear and anxiety, and write. I felt St Michael's energy so powerfully beside me during that time and I gained the courage to make the difficult decision to step back and hand the problem into the hands of Divine wisdom and love. I surrendered control and 'Let go and let God', as wise friends had counselled me. It was a time of great learning, spiritually, and I began to see that everything has a reason, although it might not be apparent at the time, and if one is open to learning the lessons that come from a difficult situation, they will turn into the most precious gifts. By learning to trust, disengaging from fear and anxiety, and holding only positive thoughts about the outcome, my anxieties faded away.

From that experience I was given a great gift that sustains me through all difficulties. That gift is there for all of us if we choose to accept it. Tough things still happen — there's no magic wand that makes troubles disappear. But when things are hard, it is easier to face them when you hand the situation over in this way. Asking for the Divine plan of your life to unfold is an affirmation of great trust, and if you can trust enough to relinquish control the rewards are great. Once you take that first step of asking, all you have to do is simply say, 'Help me,' and an abundance of aid will come.

During that time I remember most vividly how I was truly protected by St Michael and my guardian angels. Troubled and worried one day, I was driving along, fretting about how to deal with the problems that seemed insurmountable. I turned right at a junction and was only half concentrating on my driving. I failed to see a car on my left-hand side and was about to enter the left lane when he beeped loudly, frightening the life out of me. Simultaneously, it was as though another pair of hands took control of the steering wheel, wrenched it to the right and kept me in my own lane. I know it was St Michael and have never doubted from that day that I am under his protection.

I remember once, soon afterwards, a friend telling me that she was finding it hard working in a job where she was often subject to abuse from members of the public. There was one man in particular whom she feared and she was on the phone to me one day when she saw him coming towards her desk. 'Oh God, no! That man is here!' she exclaimed, and I could hear the apprehension in her voice.

'Put light around him and ask St Michael to come and stand by your side,' I urged. 'Please go and stand by her,' I asked as I put down the phone and visualised her and the man in question surrounded by a golden light.

Ten minutes later she phoned me, dumbfounded. 'You'll never guess what happened,' she said. 'I said, "St Michael, come quick and stand beside me." Then the man came and sat down as quiet as a lamb and I had him sorted in five minutes. Usually he would end up taking half an hour and rant and rave and hurl abuse at me. I can't believe it. St Michael must have come.'

'He did,' I assured her.

She has called on him many times since then and, amazingly, the difficult man has never come to her desk again, even though he still comes to the public office.

In wintertime, during storms, and when roads are icy and dangerous, it is good to call on St Michael's protection. Old people are especially vulnerable. Often when I'm driving, and I see someone struggling along, I ask St Michael to come to their aid. It's something we can all do if we see someone in difficulty, careworn or burdened.

By requesting a blessing for someone we are also receiving a blessing for ourselves because we have opened to that beautiful higher energy that surrounds us and is available to us whenever we wish. The more we tune into this wonderful energy, the more our planet will be helped. With all the wars and bombings and death and destruction that are scourging the nations of the earth at this time, it seems that our poor planet is undergoing a harsh and vicious winter. What can one person do to make a difference? one wonders despairingly. Although it can appear very much to the contrary, love will always overcome hate. If every single person could open to the energy of love by asking for a blessing for just one person on the earth, there would be a massive shift in the earth's energy. If we can see each other as equal and Divine, our outlook would change so radically that all vicious hatred would fade away. With the help of St Michael and the Angels of Winter, it is something to strive for, and so, dear reader, I ask for a blessing for you wherever you are. And if you carry heavy burdens I ask that they will be lifted from you as mine were lifted from me when I asked for help.

MERCY AND
FORGIVENESS

In January 2004, in the depths of winter, I was in the Bon Secours hospital in Glasnevin, looking out at the cold, grey, wild sky. I was waiting to find out if I was a suitable candidate for a disc fusion. The Dublin Mountains were frosted with snow and, after a while, flakes began to fall, swirling, floating, whirling, covering the fir trees and the rolling green lawns until, soon, all was a blanket of white.

I was cosy and warm under my white blankets and I felt nurtured and cherished, as always, by the kind and attentive nurses, nuns and doctors who were looking after me. The door opened and a kindly faced man with a warm smile came in and handed me a leaflet. 'You might like to read this,' he said, and then he was gone.

I looked at the leaflet and it had a picture of Jesus on it, with beautiful rays of light bursting from His heart. 'Will You Help Me?' it said. It was a leaflet about the Devotion to the Divine Mercy and a novena given to St Faustina, who was canonised by Pope John Paul II on 30 April 2000. Jesus had said to her, '*Speak to the world about My Mercy. Let all mankind recognise My unfathomable mercy.*'

I thought of how many times I'd experienced the utter compassion and mercy of Jesus in my lifetime, especially during the hard years of pain. In my hours of need, He always provided for me.

Sometimes we judge each other harshly. Often we judge ourselves most harshly. I was reminded of this when I read the poem 'Beautiful Snow', written in the voice of a forlorn young woman in dire straits, who has lost everything. But even as she judges herself, she asks, 'Is there mercy for me?'

Where there is compassion, unconditional love and mercy, there is no harsh judgement. Our generation and that of our parents and grandparents were taught of a wrathful God. We were taught we were not worthy. But by virtue of our very divinity, the divinity that comes from our creation, we are greatly worthy and we should remind ourselves of that often and be aware of the beauty of our souls and ourselves.

When I am in the winter of my life I won't fear death. That's not to say I'm not a bit apprehensive about the way of dying. Who isn't? But one of the greatest gifts that I've been given is of knowing that something wonderful awaits us and that Jesus and all the ascended masters and the angels, saints and guides will be there, overflowing with unconditional love.

In this heartfelt poem, 'Beautiful Snow', a young woman asks, 'Is there mercy for me? Will He heed my weak prayer?' and again, as with 'The Old Woman of the Roads', it's the forlorn cry – will God listen to our prayers? Sometimes we feel our prayers aren't answered, but I know now that there is a Divine plan for all our lives and we are not alone. If you imagine life as a tapestry, all we see are the threads hanging out at the back. We sometimes don't know where we're going or what we're doing, but if we could see the front of the tapestry we would see the glorious picture that is our life. We will see that picture at the end of our earthly journey and know that we are beautiful souls and that our prayers were always answered in the most perfect way.

BEAUTIFUL SNOW

Anon[*]

Oh, the snow, the beautiful snow,
Filling the sky and earth below,
Over the housetops, over the street,
Over the heads of people you meet;
Dancing – Flirting – Skimming along
Beautiful snow! It can do no wrong;
Flying to kiss a fair lady's cheek,
Clinging to lips in frolicksome freak;
Beautiful snow from Heaven above,
Pure as an angel, gentle as love!

Oh! the snow, the beautiful snow,
How the flakes gather and laugh as they go
Whirling about in maddening fun;
Chasing – Laughing – Hurrying by,
It lights on the face and it sparkles the eye;
And the dogs with a bark and a bound
Snap at the crystals as they eddy around;
The town is alive, and its heart is aglow,
To welcome the coming of beautiful snow!

How wild the crowd goes swaying along,
Hailing each other with humor and song;
How the gay sleighs like meteors flash by,
Bright for a moment, then lost to the eye;
Ringing – Swinging – Dashing they go,

Over the crest of the beautiful snow;
Snow so pure when it falls from the sky,
As to make one regret to see it lie
To be trampled and tracked by thousands of feet
Till it blends with the filth in the horrible street.

Once I was pure as the snow, but I fell,
Fell like the snow flakes from Heaven to Hell;
Fell to be trampled as filth in the street,
Fell to be scoffed, to be spit on and beat;
Pleading – Cursing – Dreading to die,
Selling my soul to whoever would buy;
Dealing in shame for a morsel of bread,
Hating the living and fearing the dead,
Merciful God! have I fallen so low!
And yet I was once like the beautiful snow.

Once I was fair as the beautiful snow,
With an eye like a crystal, a heart like its glow;
Once I was loved for my innocent grace –
Flattered and sought for the charms of my face!
Fathers – Mothers – Sisters – all,
God and myself I have lost by my fall;
The veriest wretch that goes shivering by,
Will make a wide sweep lest I wander too nigh,
For all that is on or above me I know,
There is nothing so pure as the beautiful snow.

How strange it should be that this beautiful
    snow
Should fall on a sinner with nowhere to go!

How strange it should be when the night comes
   again
If the snow and the ice struck my desperate
   brain!
Fainting – Freezing – Dying – alone,
Too wicked for prayer, too weak for a moan
To be heard in the streets of the crazy town,
Gone mad in the joy of snow coming down;
To be and to die in my terrible woe,
With a bed and a shroud of the beautiful snow.

Helpless and foul as the trampled snow,
Sinner, despair not! Christ stoopeth low
To rescue the soul that is lost in sin,
And raise it to life and enjoyment again.
Groaning – Bleeding – Dying – for thee,
The Crucified One hung on the cursed tree!
His accents of mercy fall soft on thine ear,
'Is there mercy for me? Will He heed my weak
   prayer?'
Oh God! in the stream that for sinners did flow
Wash me, and I shall be whiter than snow.

*The identity of the author is not clearly established, but the poem was first published by a 'J. W. Watson' in *Ypsilanti Commercial* on 8 January, 1870.

In a way winter is the real spring, the time when the inner things happen, the resurge of nature.

Edna O'Brien

Walls for the wind,
And a roof for the rain,
And drinks beside the fire —
Laughter to cheer you
And those you love near you,
And all that your heart may desire!

Irish blessing

HOPE

Perhaps winter's greatest blessing is the gift of hope. The cold, wet days and long, dark nights we've endured will come to an end. The earth has renewed itself and, as the days lengthen and the green buds of spring appear, spirits lift and lighten. It's a wonderful time in the cycle of nature, and in the cycle of our lives, when we emerge with hope from some grief or hardship, loss or pain that has beset us.

Without hope in our lives we would tread a long, hard, dreary path. Hope is a grace that is given to us. Even in the worst times of my life, when I was in chronic pain and beset by the difficulties it caused, I was lucky in that I always hoped there was light at the end of the tunnel. No matter how hard it is, if we can fan the little spark of hope that lies deep within us, it will sustain us and keep us going no matter what.

I've often found at difficult times in my life that I'll hear something, or read something, or someone will come to me just when I need them. At Easter 2004, when I was very down, waiting to have my operation, a lovely card came to me out of the blue. It said simply:

We believe in hope.
'Hope does not disappoint.'

(Romans v, 5)

What a lift it gave me. I felt it was a sign to look to the future with hope and to have faith that all would go well with my surgery. Today, I can say gratefully that hope was not misplaced and I am so much better. I kept that card and had it with me in hospital, and gave thanks for God's loving grace and goodness in giving me such a helping hand and enabling me to keep my fears and apprehensions at bay.

In W. B. Yeats' wonderful poem, 'To a Child Dancing in the Wind', he gives an exuberant portrayal of childhood innocence and hope, in contrast to the disillusionment of the world-weary adult.

Having been blessed with precious, gorgeous young nieces and nephews, I find it easy to be hopeful and joyful in their company. Children have so much to teach us about life and love and hope. If now and again we can try to view life through a child's eyes, it's amazing how carefree, natural and uninhibited we can become.

I remember taking my one of my nieces to the Botanic Gardens in Glasnevin late one autumn. She was three at the time and her excitement at seeing great drifts of crispy red, russet and golden leaves under the trees was unbounded. How she danced and leapt with giddy glee. What could I do but join in? We had wonderful, innocent fun. Another time, when we were lighting a candle in the church, she turned to me and said quite earnestly, pointing to a statue with a very large halo, 'Tricia, why does that man have a bicycle wheel on his head?' I'm sure God and all the saints had a great laugh; I certainly did. To children, anything is possible and in Florence Scovel-Shinn's bestselling metaphysical book, *The Game of Life and How to Play It*, she writes of hope and of how 'Faith is the substance of things hoped for, the evidence of things not seen.'

In Padraic Colum's deeply evocative and moving poem, 'The Old Woman of the Roads', the tired, weary old woman tells us how she is praying to God on high for a home of her own. By her very act of faith in praying to God she is showing hope. I like to think of her, snug in her little house, her prayers answered. In Shelley's 'Ode to the West Wind' he gives us that wonderful, memorable line: 'If Winter comes, can Spring be far behind?'

As long as we have hope we are rich, and my wish for you, dear reader, is that all the things you hope for will come to you and enrich you in mind, body, soul and divinity.

We grow great by dreams. All big men are dreamers. They see things in the soft haze of a spring day or in the red fire of a long winter's evening. Some of us let these great dreams die, but others nourish and protect them.

Woodrow Wilson

TO A CHILD DANCING IN THE WIND

W. B. Yeats

Dance there upon the shore;
What need have you to care
For wind or water's roar?
And tumble out your hair
That the salt drops have wet;
Being young you have not known
The fool's triumph, nor yet
Love lost as soon as won,
Nor the best labourer dead
And all the sheaves to bind.
What need have you to dread
The monstrous crying of wind?

Excerpt from

THE SEASONS: WINTER

James Thomson

See, Winter comes to rule the varied year,
Sullen and sad, with all his rising train –
Vapours, and clouds, and storms. Be these my theme,
These, that exalt the soul to solemn thought
And heavenly musing. Welcome, kindred glooms!
Congenial horrors, hail! With frequent foot,
Pleas'd have I, in my cheerful morn of life,
When nurs'd by careless solitude I liv'd
And sung of Nature with unceasing joy,
Pleas'd have I wander'd through your rough domain;
Trod the pure virgin-snows, myself as pure;
Heard the winds roar, and the big torrent burst;
Or seen the deep-fermenting tempest brew'd
In the grim evening-sky. Thus pass'd the time,
Till through the lucid chambers of the south
Look'd out the joyous Spring – look'd out and
    smil'd.

THE OLD WOMAN
OF THE ROADS

Padraic Colum

Oh, to have a little house!
To own the hearth and stool and all!
The heaped-up sods against the fire,
The pile of turf against the wall!

To have a clock with weights and chains
And pendulum swinging up and down!
A dresser filled with shining delph,
Speckled and white and blue and brown!

I could be busy all the day
Clearing and sweeping hearth and floor
And fixing on their shelf again
My white and blue and speckled store!

I could be there at night
Beside the fire and by myself,
Sure of a bed and loth to leave
The ticking clock and shining delph!

Oh! But I'm weary of mist and dark,
And roads where there's never a house or bush,
And tired I am of the bog, and the road,
And the crying wind and the lonesome hush!

And I'm praying to God on High,
And I am praying Him night and day,
For a little house – a house of my own –
Out of the wind's and the rain's way.

ODE TO THE WEST WIND

Percy Bysshe Shelley

My spirit! Be thou me, impetuous one!
Drive my dead thoughts over the universe
Like withered leaves to quicken a new birth!
And, by the incantation of this verse,
Scatter, as from an unextinguished hearth
Ashes and sparks, my words among mankind!
Be through my lips to unawakened earth
The trumpet of a prophecy! O Wind,
If Winter comes, can Spring be far behind?

May the saddest day of your future be no worse
Than the happiest day of your past.

Irish blessing

Remember always that you are just a visitor here, a traveller passing through. Your stay is but short and the moment of your departure unknown.

None can live without toil and a craft that provides your needs is a blessing indeed. But if you toil without rest, fatigue and weariness will overtake you, and you will be denied the joy that comes from labour's end.

Speak quietly and kindly and be not forward with either opinions or advice. If you talk much, this will make you deaf to what others say, and you should know that there are few so wise that they cannot learn from others.

Be near when help is needed, but far when praise and thanks are being offered.

Take small account of might, wealth and fame, for they soon pass and are forgotten. Instead, nurture love within you and strive to be a friend to all. Truly, compassion is a balm for many wounds.

Treasure silence when you find it, and while being mindful of your duties, set time aside, to be alone with yourself.

Cast off pretence and self-deception and see yourself as you really are.

Despite all appearances, no one is really evil. They are led astray by ignorance. If you ponder this truth always you will offer more light, rather than blame and condemnation.

You, no less than all beings have Buddha Nature within. Your essential Mind is pure. Therefore, when defilements cause you to stumble and fall, let not remorse nor dark foreboding cast you down. Be of good cheer and with this understanding, summon strength and walk on.

Faith is like a lamp and wisdom makes the flame burn bright. Carry this lamp always and in good time the darkness will yield and you will abide in the Light.

Dhammavadaka Sutra
Buddhist blessing

Winter has been a powerful season in my life, a season of self-discovery and knowledge and, ultimately, great spiritual riches. It's a wonderful gift to have that sustaining spiritual dimension to my life. Something that was missing has been found and, where I thought doors had closed on me, I soon came to realise that many more had opened. Dear reader, may your winters be as enriching as mine and may you always receive the abundance of the universe.